Lyrics Journal:

Songwriter's Notebook

4ᵗʰ & Main Books

Music:

Song Title:_____
Inspiration:

_____

_____

_____

_____

Lyrics:

_____
_____
_____
_____
_____
_____
_____
_____
_____
_____
_____
_____
_____
_____
_____
_____
_____
_____
_____
_____
_____
_____

Music:

Song Title:_____
Inspiration:

_____

_____

_____

_____

Lyrics:

_____
_____
_____
_____
_____
_____
_____
_____
_____
_____
_____
_____
_____
_____
_____
_____
_____
_____
_____

Music:

Song Title:_____

Inspiration:

_____

_____

_____

_____

Lyrics:

Music:

Song Title:_____
Inspiration:

_____

_____

_____

_____

Lyrics:

_____
_____
_____
_____
_____
_____
_____
_____
_____
_____
_____
_____
_____
_____
_____
_____
_____
_____
_____
_____
_____
_____
_____
_____

Music:

Song Title:_____

Inspiration:

_____

_____

_____

_____

Lyrics:

_____
_____
_____
_____
_____
_____
_____
_____
_____
_____
_____
_____
_____
_____
_____
_____
_____
_____

Music:

Song Title:_____

Inspiration:

_____

_____

_____

_____

Lyrics:

_____
_____
_____
_____
_____
_____
_____
_____
_____
_____
_____
_____
_____
_____
_____
_____
_____
_____
_____
_____
_____
_____
_____

Music:

Song Title:_____
Inspiration:

_____

_____

_____

_____

Lyrics:

_____
_____
_____
_____
_____
_____
_____
_____
_____
_____
_____
_____
_____
_____
_____
_____
_____
_____
_____

Music:

Song Title:_____
Inspiration:

_____

_____

_____

_____

Lyrics:

_____
_____
_____
_____
_____
_____
_____
_____
_____
_____
_____
_____
_____
_____
_____
_____
_____

Music:

Song Title:_____
Inspiration:

_____

_____

_____

_____

Lyrics:

_____
_____
_____
_____
_____
_____
_____
_____
_____
_____
_____
_____
_____
_____
_____
_____
_____
_____
_____
_____
_____

Music :

Song Title:_____
Inspiration:

_____

_____

_____

_____

Lyrics:

_____
_____
_____
_____
_____
_____
_____
_____
_____
_____
_____
_____
_____
_____
_____
_____
_____
_____
_____
_____
_____
_____

Music :

Song Title:_____

Inspiration:

_____

_____

_____

_____

Lyrics:

_____
_____
_____
_____
_____
_____
_____
_____
_____
_____
_____
_____
_____
_____
_____
_____
_____
_____
_____
_____
_____
_____
_____
_____

Music:

Song Title:_____

Inspiration:

_____

_____

_____

_____

Lyrics:

_____
_____
_____
_____
_____
_____
_____
_____
_____
_____
_____
_____
_____
_____
_____
_____
_____
_____
_____
_____
_____
_____

Music:

Song Title:_____

Inspiration:

_____

_____

_____

_____

Lyrics:

_____
_____
_____
_____
_____
_____
_____
_____
_____
_____
_____
_____
_____
_____
_____
_____
_____
_____
_____

Music:

Song Title:_____
Inspiration:

_____

_____

_____

_____

Lyrics:

_____
_____
_____
_____
_____
_____
_____
_____
_____
_____
_____
_____
_____
_____
_____
_____
_____
_____
_____
_____
_____

Music :

Song Title:_____
Inspiration:

_____

_____

_____

_____

Lyrics:

_____
_____
_____
_____
_____
_____
_____
_____
_____
_____
_____
_____
_____
_____
_____
_____
_____
_____
_____
_____
_____
_____
_____
_____
_____
_____
_____

Music:

Song Title:_____
Inspiration:

_____

_____

_____

_____

Lyrics:

_____
_____
_____
_____
_____
_____
_____
_____
_____
_____
_____
_____
_____
_____
_____
_____
_____
_____
_____
_____
_____
_____
_____
_____
_____

Music:

Song Title:_____

Inspiration:

_____

_____

_____

_____

Lyrics:

_____
_____
_____
_____
_____
_____
_____
_____
_____
_____
_____
_____
_____
_____
_____
_____
_____
_____
_____
_____
_____
_____

Music:

Song Title:_____

Inspiration:

_____

_____

_____

_____

Lyrics:

_____
_____
_____
_____
_____
_____
_____
_____
_____
_____
_____
_____
_____
_____
_____
_____
_____
_____
_____
_____
_____

Music:

Song Title:_____
Inspiration:

_____

_____

_____

_____

Lyrics:

_____
_____
_____
_____
_____
_____
_____
_____
_____
_____
_____
_____
_____
_____
_____
_____
_____
_____
_____
_____
_____
_____
_____
_____

Music:

Song Title:_____
Inspiration:

_____

_____

_____

_____

Lyrics:

_____
_____
_____
_____
_____
_____
_____
_____
_____
_____
_____
_____
_____
_____
_____
_____
_____
_____
_____

Music:

Song Title:_____

Inspiration:

_____

_____

_____

_____

Lyrics:

_____
_____
_____
_____
_____
_____
_____
_____
_____
_____
_____
_____
_____
_____
_____
_____
_____
_____
_____